WILD PLACES

THE LIFE OF NATURALIST DAVID ATTENBOROUGH

HAYLEY ROCCO · JOHN ROCCO CALDECOTT HONOREE

putnam

G. P. PUTNAM'S SONS

"If we take care of nature,
nature will take care of us."

—David Attenborough

This is our planet.

On our planet,
there are 8.7 million
types of animals.

One of those types
is human, and one
of those humans
is a man named David.

When David was born, more than two-thirds
of our planet was covered in wild places.
That was where most of the animals lived.

The other third was where the humans lived.

As David grew, he liked
to explore the wild places
near his home in England.

On one of his adventures, he
broke open a rock and discovered
the fossil of an ammonite inside.

Ammonites were sea creatures that
had died off millions of years ago.

It thrilled David to know that he was
the first human to see *this* particular
animal. He found many others,
and his curiosity grew.

"Why were there so
many different kinds
of ammonites?"

David went back to the wild places
often to see what else he might discover.
He loved collecting fossils, rocks, newts,
and other things.

When he grew older, David went to a university to learn more
about the wild places and the things that lived there.
Understanding how the natural world worked
was more important to him than studying politics,
languages, or the history of queens and kings.

And the more he discovered,
the more David wanted to share
what he had learned with others.

Just as television was becoming popular, David began working on a nature program. Each week, he introduced viewers to many different kinds of animals that were brought in from the zoo. His passionate explanations captivated people of all ages.

"This extraordinary creature is half-blind, half-deaf, and this is just about as fast as it can move."

One day, David had an idea. If they filmed the program *in* the wild places, he could show us where and how these animals lived!

So David started traveling all over the planet, filming animals in wild places most people had never seen before. He became our connection to the natural world.

Through David, we met gorillas high up in the mountains of Africa.

We played with penguins on icebergs in Antarctica.

We cuddled with sloths in the
rain forests of South America.

And we listened to the songs
of humpback whales in
the South Pacific.

Over the years,
David's programs have
been enjoyed by millions
of people around the world.

But as time went on, David noticed that
the wild places were shrinking, while
the not-so-wild places kept on expanding.

"We are replacing
the wild with the tame."

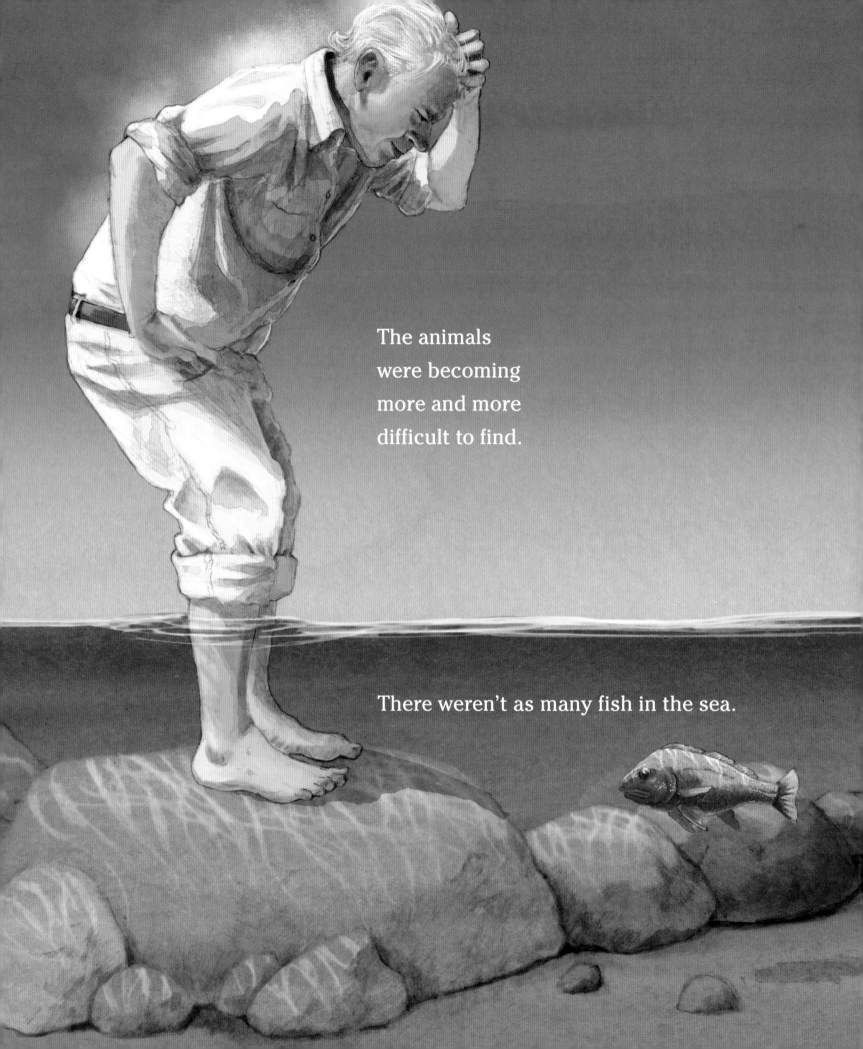

The animals
were becoming
more and more
difficult to find.

There weren't as many fish in the sea.

There weren't as
many birds in the sky.

David also noticed that the weather was becoming more unpredictable. There were bigger storms, extreme flooding, uncontrollable wildfires, and longer droughts.

The natural world he cared for was in trouble.
Humankind was in danger too.

David was worried. He talked
with scientists and other experts
to find out why this was happening.
He learned that it was connected
to the loss of wild places.

He realized he had to share
what he'd learned and what
we needed to do to fix it.

"We must rewild
the world.
If we act now,
we can yet
put it right."

So David made new programs. He showed
us how our old ways of getting energy
are destroying the planet.

"We will have to use new ways to get the energy we need—from the sun, the wind, and our powerful rivers and tides."

He explained how overfishing
is hurting our oceans.

"If there are no-fishing zones in the oceans, sea life will have time to recover and grow."

He showed us how much land it takes
to raise animals for their meat.

"If we eat less meat, there will be more land for wild places."

And he helped us understand the importance of protecting our forests.

"We need our forests to clean the air and provide a home to more wild animals."

David has spent his lifetime
showing us how every living thing
on this planet is connected.

And David has hope that
if we all do our part . . .

. . . together we can
bring back the wild places.

AUTHOR'S NOTE

SIR DAVID ATTENBOROUGH is a world-renowned broadcaster, documentary filmmaker, naturalist, and author. Over the course of seven decades, he has written, produced, and presented hundreds of natural history programs for millions of viewers.

The middle of three sons, David was born in London on May 8, 1926, and grew up in nearby Leicester, England, where his father was the president of University College, Leicester. His mother also worked at the college as a secretary and philanthropist.

In 1947, David earned a degree in natural sciences from Clare College, Cambridge. Soon after, he was called to serve in the Royal Navy for two years. In 1952, he applied for a job as a radio producer for the British Broadcasting Company.

PA Images / Alamy Stock Photo

While he didn't land that position, he was offered a role in the BBC television division. Television, a new medium at the time, offered David the unique opportunity to innovate different types of programming.

He began working on a show with naturalist Julian Huxley called *The Pattern of Animals*, where they introduced viewers to animals from the local London Zoo. There, he met Jack Lester, the curator for the zoo's reptile house. Together they decided it would be more interesting to film animals in their natural environment. With the advent of commercial air travel in the 1950s, they could travel to remote locations and record exotic creatures in their own habitats. Originally, Jack Lester was going to present the animals on the program, but because of an illness, David stepped in and hosted the first broadcast, which aired in 1954. The series was called *Zoo Quest*, and it ran on BBC until 1963, becoming the most popular nature series in Great Britain.

From there, David went on to create hundreds of documentaries. His hit series *Life on Earth* had over 500 million viewers worldwide. His many other programs—including *The Living Planet*, *The Trials of Life*, *The Private Life of Plants*, *The Life of Birds*, *The Blue Planet*, *The Life of Mammals*, *Planet Earth*, and *Life in Cold Blood*—became hugely popular as well. David's narration is so recognizable that he's commonly referred to as "the voice of nature."

Additionally, throughout his career, David has been instrumental in protecting animals and their habitats, working closely with organizations like Fauna & Flora International, the Conservation Volunteers, and the World Land Trust. He has received countless honors for his environmental work, including the prestigious World Wildlife Fund Duke of Edinburgh Conservation Award.

imageBROKER / Alamy Stock Photo

Over the years, more than a dozen animals and plants have been named in David's honor. He has been knighted twice—first in 1985 and again in 2022—for his contributions to television broadcasting and conservation. He has received thirty-two honorary degrees from universities all over Great Britain and has won dozens of awards over the course of his career, including five Emmys.

In 2020, at the age of ninety-four, David released *A Life on Our Planet: My Witness Statement and Vision for the Future*, a book and a film of the same title. These works exposed readers and viewers alike to David's observations of the decline of wild places on Earth throughout his lifetime. But, in David's singular style, he offers hope that if we act now, we can make positive change and restore the health of our planet for all living things, including humankind.

SELECTED BIBLIOGRAPHY

BOOKS

Attenborough, David. *Adventures of a Young Naturalist*. Great Britain: Two Roads, 2017.

Attenborough, David. *Journeys to the Other Side of the World: Further Adventures of a Young Naturalist*. Great Britain: Two Roads, 2018.

Attenborough, David. *Zoo Quest for a Dragon: Including the Quest for the Paradise Birds*. London: Lutterworth Press, 1957.

Attenborough, David. *Zoo Quest to Guiana*. London: Lutterworth Press, 1956.

Attenborough, David, with Jonnie Hughes. *A Life on Our Planet: My Witness Statement and a Vision for the Future*. New York: Grand Central Publishing, Hachette Book Group, 2020.

DOCUMENTARIES

Attenborough, David, dir. *The Life of Mammals*. Episode 3, "Plant Predators." BBC Natural History/Discovery Channel UK, 2002.

Fothergill, Alastair, Jonnie Hughes, and Keith Scholey, dirs. *David Attenborough: A Life on Our Planet*. Altitude Film Entertainment, Silverback Films, World Wildlife Fund, 2020.

SOURCE NOTES

All the quotes in this book were taken from the film *David Attenborough: A Life on Our Planet*, except for the quote "This extraordinary creature is half-blind, half-deaf, and this is just about as fast as it can move," which was taken from the documentary series *The Life of Mammals*, episode 3, "Plant Predators."

REWILDING OUR PLANET

All living things on Earth, including humans, inhabit complex networks called ecosystems, where animals, plants, and other life depend on one another and the natural environment for survival. Healthy ecosystems provide clean food, water, and air; enrich our soil; and regulate the climate. Scientists have found that biodiversity—or the variety of life—is the key to a healthy ecosystem.

Unfortunately, the perfect balance of nature is being destroyed. Our planet is getting warmer because of something called climate change, or long-term shifts in temperatures and weather patterns. When the climate changes even a few degrees, ecosystems suffer because plants, animals, and other life aren't able to adapt. This may cause some to die off, while others may flourish, disrupting the balance that keeps these ecosystems healthy. Additionally, warmer oceans and air cause worsening weather crises, like storms, droughts, floods, and wildfires.

What causes climate change? Scientists agree our planet is warming due to human activities.

The methods in which humans have sourced food, energy, and land—especially in wealthy countries like the United States—have critically endangered our planet. Fortunately, some ways that we can obtain these things are sustainable, or causing minimal damage to the environment and using fewer natural resources. If we take action now, we can stop the damage we have done and even restore the balance to our planet.

Rewilding the world means protecting and reviving natural areas—such as forests, grasslands, and coral reefs—to bring back biodiversity and restore healthy ecosystems. Throughout the world, scientists, conservationists, environmentalists, and volunteers are working to save existing wild places, safeguard animals and plants critical to those ecosystems, and revitalize exhausted and overused land.

There is hope for our planet if we all work together alongside nature and embrace the fact that we, too, are a part of the natural world.

> "It's surely our responsibility to do everything within our power to create a planet that provides a home not just for us, but for all life on Earth."
>
> —David Attenborough

WHAT CAN YOU DO TO HELP? It may seem like many of the problems and solutions on the next page are out of your control, and in some ways, that is true. While reducing, reusing, and recycling is a great start, most of these problems need to be solved through new laws at the local, state, national, and even global level.

The people who make these laws need to hear your voice. You can write to your congressional representatives and ask for change. The more people who do this, the more likely they will create laws that will protect our planet.

For more resources and to find out how to write your congressperson, go to **MeetTheWildThings.com**.

FOSSIL FUELS: Over the past 150 years, the population of humans on Earth has grown and our need for energy has increased. Fossil fuels like coal, oil, and gas have been our primary sources of energy. But mining and burning these fuels releases colossal amounts of greenhouse gases— such as carbon dioxide, methane, nitrous oxide, and water vapor— into our atmosphere, which traps the heat from our sun, leading to global warming and climate change.

RENEWABLE ENERGY: Nature can provide us with an endless supply of energy from sources like the sun, the wind, and rivers and tides. We have started to harness this power using solar farms, wind farms, and hydroelectric plants. These sources are called "clean energy" because they emit little or no pollution or greenhouse gases.

OVERFISHING: Seafood is an important food source for humans. But if we take too much from the ocean, fish do not have a chance to reproduce and replenish their populations. If we continue to deplete the ocean of fish, many species critical to the health of the largest ecosystem on the planet will go extinct.

PROTECTING OUR OCEANS: We need to change the way we harvest fish from the oceans by monitoring fish populations and limiting catches. Currently, only 7 percent of our oceans are protected from fishing. If more of the ocean was off-limits, fish would have more protected space to thrive. Studies have shown that in protected areas, fish populations rebound to such a degree that they spill over into areas where they can be fished sustainably.

LARGE-SCALE FARMING: Large-scale farming grows most of our food, including animals for meat, using large swaths of land and chemical pesticides and fertilizers. These chemicals pollute the water, destroy the biodiversity that helps maintain the land, and eventually deplete the soil. Beef cattle also release massive amounts of methane, a greenhouse gas, into the atmosphere, which contributes to climate change.

SUSTAINABLE FARMING AND EATING LESS BEEF: We have the ability to create farms that can be sustainable ecosystems. These farms can manage water more wisely, build healthy soil, prevent erosion, and promote biodiversity. Also, if we all eat less red meat, demand for it will decrease. This will lower the impact raising beef cattle will have on our planet.

DEFORESTATION: Our forests not only provide homes for 80 percent of the wild animals on our planet, but trees also absorb carbon dioxide, a greenhouse gas. When we cut down our forests, we have fewer trees to capture carbon dioxide, resulting in global warming. We also lose the biodiverse ecosystems that live in those forests.

CHANGING HOW WE CONSUME: Our forests are disappearing because of our demand for products like beef, palm oil, timber, and soy. If we become more aware of the products we use and the quantity we buy—and how they are raised or grown—together we can reduce deforestation.

For Wendy Hapgood and John Steward
of Wild Tomorrow, who risked everything
to help wildlife and wild places in South Africa.
You serve as an inspiration that we can all do
our part for the greater good of the planet.

—H.R. and J.R.

ACKNOWLEDGMENTS First, our immense gratitude goes to David Attenborough for inspiring generations of humans to explore, discover, care for, and cherish the natural world we live in. Thank you for being a pillar of hope for us all. Special thanks to Dr. Justin Kirkpatrick, Environmental Economist, Michigan State University, for taking the time to verify the climate change information throughout the book, and to Elizabeth Rusch for her guidance on how to connect with our congresspeople to invoke change. Thank you also to Tori Gray, Greg Canning, Kevin Jolliffe, and the entire team of Wild Tomorrow, for effectively expanding wild places for the betterment of wildlife and our world. An extra-special thanks to our team at G. P. Putnam's Sons Books for Young Readers, including editor Stephanie Pitts, art director Cecilia Yung, designer Nicole Rheingans, and publisher Jennifer Klonsky, for not only taking on this project, but for seeing its potential and making it a better book than we could have imagined. And of course, our immense thanks to our wonderful agent and dear friend Rob Weisbach, who has a heart of gold.

Library of Congress Cataloging-in-Publication Data • Names: Rocco, Hayley, author. | Rocco, John, illustrator. • Title: Wild places: the life of naturalist David Attenborough / written by Hayley Rocco; illustrated by John Rocco. • Description: New York: G. P. Putnam's Sons, an imprint of Penguin Random House LLC, 2023. Summary: "A nonfiction account of the life of British naturalist David Attenborough and his advocacy for the protection of wild places on Earth"—Provided by publisher. Identifiers: LCCN 2022055545 (print) | LCCN 2022055546 (ebook) ISBN 9780593618097 (hardcover) | ISBN 9780593618110 (kindle edition) | ISBN 9780593618103 Subjects: LCSH: Attenborough, David, 1926– —Juvenile literature. Naturalists—Great Britain—Biography—Juvenile literature. | Television personalities—Great Britain—Biography—Juvenile literature. • Classification: LCC QH31.A765 R63 2023 (print) | LCC QH31.A765 (ebook) | DDC 508.092—dc23/eng/20230113 LC record available at https://lccn.loc.gov/2022055545 • LC ebook record available at https://lccn.loc.gov/2022055546

Manufactured in China • ISBN 9780593618097 • 10 9 8 7 6 5 4 3 2 1
TOPL

Design by Nicole Rheingans • Text set in ITC Cheltenham Pro • The art was created with pencil, watercolor and digital paint.
The publisher does not have any control over and does not assume any responsibility for author or third-party websites or their content.